D0010935

Table of Contents

Foreword
By Phil Jackson

The Power of Double-Goal Coaching, Jim Thompson's latest book, is a terrific, concise summary of the impact a character-focused coach can have – for a season or a lifetime.

It is a practical book coaches can use to get better results from players while providing an ethically superior approach to competitive sports. When coaches regularly use these positive forms of motivation, they find they have willing, eager athletes on their teams.

In particular, our coaches, parents, and athletes need to understand and embrace what Jim calls the ROOTS of Honoring the Game: respect for Rules, Opponents, Officials, Teammates, and Self. Honoring the Game is needed at all levels of sports.

Rules exist so games can be played and officiated fairly. We expect coaches to follow the rules and not find ways to bend the rules. Doing so, we honor the spirit of playing the game. Opponents should be respected, not ridiculed. Positive Coaching Alliance believes that in honoring the opponents, you recognize that worthy opposition is a gift that forces you to play to your highest ability.

I have personal experience with how honoring the opponent is a concept that works. In 1990, my Chicago Bulls were defeated for the third consecutive time by the Detroit Pistons. We had lost to them in the first round, the second round, and in the finals of the Eastern Conference playoffs. It was easy to build up dislike for the Pistons "Bad Boys" after such futility. Each year had brought a confrontation, from a bench-clearing brawl to take-downs and flagrant fouls, one of which resulted in a concussion to our young star, Scottie Pippen.

THE POWER OF DOUBLE-GOAL COACHING

Developing Winners in Sports and Life

By Jim Thompson

BALANCE SPORTS PUBLISHING

Balance Sports Publishing, LLC · Portola Valley, California

Balance Sports Publishing, LLC
195 Lucero Way
Portola Valley, CA 94028
(650) 561-9586

LIBRARY OF CONGRESS CATALOG-IN-PRINTING DATA
Thompson, Jim, 1949-
    The power of double-goal coaching : developing winners in sports and life / by Jim Thompson. — 1st ed.

        p. ; cm.

    ISBN: 978-0-9821317-4-9

1. Sports for children--Coaching. 2. Sports for children--Psychological aspects. 3. Coaching (Athletics) I. Title.

GV709.24 .T56 2010
796/.077

FIRST EDITION
Printed in the United States of America

12 11 10 9 8 7 6 5   21 20 19 18 17 16 15 14

Balance Sports Publishing, LLC and the author disclaim responsibility for adverse effects or consequences from the misapplication or injudicious use of the information contained in this book. Mention of resources and associations does not imply endorsement by Balance Sports Publishing, LLC or the author.

Designed by Elisa Tanaka

Special thanks to the "brain trust" of coaches that helped inform this book:
Eric Eisendrath, Jeaney Garcia, Molly Hellerman, Ray Lokar, Courtney Pollack, Jason Sacks, Joe Scally, Tina Syer, Joe Thomas, and Kathy Toon.

As a result, we had developed a raw anger toward their team that had clouded our abilities to function instinctively as a team. I used something I'd learned from the Lakota of the Dakotas. They had a mortal enemy in the Crow, but they honored them because they were wonderful warriors and to fight against the Crow demanded bravery, cunning, and teamwork. I borrowed that theme. The conflict brought about the best of both tribes. So rather than getting angry and frustrated in a contest with a physically stronger team like the Pistons, and flailing out in futility, we resorted to meeting them with focused willpower, resilience, and teamwork. We honored the Pistons ability to compete and it worked in our favor, with six NBA championships for the Bulls.

I agreed to be the National Spokesperson for PCA when Jim Thompson asked me because I believe so strongly in the kind of sports culture that PCA is fighting for. I am proud of the 10 NBA championship rings that I have earned as a coach, but I also want the success of PCA to be part of my legacy.

As a leader, coach, parent, or athlete, I hope you will make it part of your legacy also. Together let's transform youth sports to be all it should be in the lives of our nation's youth.

Phil Jackson
PCA National Spokesperson
Head Coach, Los Angeles Lakers

CHAPTER ONE

Your Legacy as a Coach

I sometimes open coaching workshops by asking coaches to write or talk about the best coach they ever had and what made him or her so terrific. The stories that come out of this experience are wonderful and poignant. Often these adults are remembering things about coaches who are long dead. They describe coaches who are wise, encouraging, gentle, disciplined, great teachers, and wonderful human beings who cared about them as individuals, not just athletes who could make them look good.

These stories speak to the power of a positive coach.

Unfortunately, most of the participants also recall less pleasant experiences with coaches who failed to live up to those standards, coaches who made playing sports a miserable experience.

Coaches, both good and bad, matter. At their best they make a lifetime of difference. This begs a question worth considering: what impact will you have on the kids you coach?

I Became a Coach

I got into coaching without much thought, almost by accident. I was not tempted to try coaching when my six-year-old son decided to play soccer because that was a sport about which I knew nothing. But when basketball and baseball seasons came around, it was a different story. I had played both sports, and after watching other coaches for a year, it didn't take much to get me to agree to coach. After all, how hard could it be?

To my surprise, I discovered that coaching kids is a lot more difficult than I anticipated. I wondered…

- how to deal with parents who were on their children constantly
- how to work with co-coaches who had very different ideas about coaching
- how to corral the energy of a dozen kids with varying abilities, attention spans, and temperaments
- how to keep a strong team from becoming arrogant and ungracious with teams they easily defeated
- how to keep a weak team from getting so down in the dumps after a long losing streak that they quit giving their best effort
- how to convey the joy and love of sports to kids who seemed to be under so much pressure

This was years before PCA popularized the term "Teachable Spirit," but I had it. I enthusiastically threw myself into coaching. I read books, watched videos, went to coaching clinics, and queried other coaches non-stop. I was a sponge who couldn't learn enough about how to be a good coach. I also had an important, positive advantage.

The Power of Positivity

I came to youth sports with a bias based on my personal experience – that positive worked better. I had seen it work in classrooms with both "normal" and behavior-problem children.

My experience working with troubled kids in the Behavioral Learning Center (BLC) in St. Paul, Minnesota was formative in my thinking about positive coaching. BLC Principal Shirley Pearl and social worker Don Challman drilled into me the power of "relentless positivity" in transforming the behavior of these troubled kids. My exposure to Grace Pilon's "Workshop Way" method of welcoming mistakes – rather than fearing them – as a normal and healthy part of the learning process further influenced me.

When I began coaching, I found out that being positive with players caused them to try hard, rapidly develop new skills, and be flexible and open to new ways to accomplish their goals. Furthermore, we won a lot on the scoreboard and all of us – players, coaches, and parents – had a lot of fun. Parents wanted their kids on my team because they saw the results of a relentlessly positive approach.

When I coached high school basketball, the pattern repeated. Positive got results. Negative made things worse.

Later I found that research validated my personal experience that, for example, individuals who are treated positively solve problems better and more quickly than individuals who are not.

Barbara Fredrickson, in a landmark paper entitled *What Good Are Positive Emotions?*, says "…positive emotions serve to broaden an individual's momentary thought-action repertoire, which in turn has the effect of building that individual's physical, intellectual, and social resources."

I love Fredrickson's statement because sports is chock full of situations that require thought-action in a moment. And who doesn't want people on their team with increased physical, intellectual, and social resources?

The False Promise of Negativity

But my positive approach went against the norm of sports where negativity, against all the evidence, reigned.

We know that negativity tends to narrow attention, restrict the flow of information, and cause "threat rigidity," the tendency to become inflexible in making decisions. Negativity also poisons relationships on teams, in organizations, in families, and among friends. Regrettably, negativity by coaches transforms what should be the source of a lifelong love affair into a joyless experience that drives many kids out of sports. In fact, studies indicate that the highest rates of participation in sports occur at age 10, and that nearly 70 percent of youth sports participants drop out of sports altogether by age 13.

Nonetheless, unrestrained expression of negativity by coaches – exemplified by the "screamer" coach – is accepted, justified, and even lauded. I started Positive Coaching Alliance partly to counteract this wrong-headed and harmful approach.

My close up view of youth sports troubled me. I watched well-meaning adults working with young athletes in self-defeating ways. I saw parents and coaches who interacted with kids in ways that were virtually guaranteed to have bad results. These adults were often unwittingly blind to the fact that the primary reasons kids play sports is for fun, friends, and improvement. I saw too many coaches lose sight of what I believe is the ultimate measure of success as a youth coach – whether kids returned to play the following season.

I learned that by remaining positive and constructive with players through rain or shine a coach will get more from them. A coach who can have hard conversations with kids while remaining positive and optimistic will be more likely to help them improve. And a coach who establishes a positive team culture will help young people develop a passion for the game and be remembered by players long after they have moved on to other things.

And validation comes not only from research but from the highest levels of coaching. Phil Jackson, PCA's National Spokesperson and winner of 10 NBA titles, said: "Jim Thompson states that his positive coaching tactic may not work on a professional level. Being a believer in motivation through support and praise, I know it works at this level, too."

Transforming Youth Sports

These experiences were the seeds of Positive Coaching Alliance (PCA), a movement I started at the Stanford Department of Athletics in 1998. Since then, PCA has partnered with more than a thousand youth sports organizations and high schools, serving more than three million youth athletes across the country, in pursuit of our mission: *to transform youth sports so sports can transform youth.*

PCA's goal is to change the culture of youth sports so every

- Coach is a **Double-Goal Coach**® who prepares athletes to win and teaches life lessons through sports

- Athlete aspires to be a **Triple-Impact Competitor**™ who makes self, teammates, and the game better

- Sports parent becomes a **Second-Goal Parent**™ who concentrates on the child's character development while letting athletes and coaches focus on the first goal of winning on the scoreboard

This vision is shared by a growing number of prominent coaches, athletes, and youth sports experts who comprise PCA's National Advisory Board, including:

- **Jennifer Azzi,** Olympic gold medalist, Basketball
- **Dusty Baker,** Manager, Cincinnati Reds
- **Shane Battier,** Houston Rockets
- **Larry Brown,** Hall of Fame Basketball Coach
- **Nadia Comaneci,** Olympic gold medalist, Gymnastics
- **Bart Conner,** Olympic gold medalist, Gymnastics
- **Joan Duda,** Sports Psychology Professor, University of Birmingham, England
- **Carol Dweck,** Author of *Mindset: The New Psychology of Success*
- **Joe Ehrmann,** Founder, Coach for America
- **Joy Fawcett,** Olympic gold medalist, Soccer
- **Julie Foudy,** Olympic gold medalist, Soccer
- **Chip Heath,** Co-Author of *Made to Stick* and *Switch*
- **Phil Jackson,** Head Coach, Los Angeles Lakers
- **Ronnie Lott,** Member, National Football League Hall of Fame
- **Dot Richardson,** Olympic gold medalist, Softball
- **Doc Rivers,** Head Coach, Boston Celtics
- **Summer Sanders,** Olympic gold medalist, Swimming
- **Dean Smith,** Member, Basketball Hall of Fame
- **Doug Wilson,** General Manager, San Jose Sharks

Your Coaching Legacy

This book is the result of my own coaching journey as well as the combined knowledge of hundreds of coaches and athletes who make up the Positive Coaching Alliance.

Whether you coach pee-wees or high school varsity, in rec leagues or elite clubs, the research-based tools and frameworks and best practices in the following chapters are designed to help you become the kind of coach whose players can't wait to come to practice, who work hard and encourage each other, and who are sad when the season is over. You'll learn unequivocally that Double-Goal Coaching and winning go hand-in-hand.

I can think of no more powerful legacy than helping young people realize their potential as people as well as athletes. That is the essence of Double-Goal Coaching. Sports can be one of the greatest teachers of life lessons and character, particularly when coaches do things the right way. I hope you will be the kind of coach your players will remember with gratefulness for the rest of their lives, even long after you have passed on.

CHAPTER TWO

The Double-Goal Coach

Few people have had as much success in sports and business as Peter Ueberroth. In 1984 he chaired the successful Los Angeles Olympic Games. Later, he was named Commissioner of Major League Baseball. In my first meeting with Peter, he said: "A coach was responsible for me going to college. Ken Stanger, my swimming and water polo coach at Fremont High School (Sunnyvale, CA), saw that I could throw well and got me to come out for water polo. He helped me get a scholarship to play at San Jose State. Without him, I doubt I would have gone to college."

We've Always Had Double-Goal Coaches

While the term Double-Goal Coach may be new, the concept is not. We have always had terrific high school and youth coaches, like Ken Stanger, who see their dual goals: helping athletes succeed in life as well as win on the scoreboard.

Double-Goal Coaches never lose sight of the unique opportunity they have to use sports to teach important aspects of life, such as hard work, fair play, teamwork, resilience, delayed gratification, and how to compete fiercely and with class. They also recognize their enormous potential to impact the course of lives, often more so than any other adult in athletes' lives other than parents. They realize their words and actions – even a single word or single action – good or bad, might be remembered for a lifetime.

But today's relentless marketing of professional sports, reinforced by 24/7 media coverage, has elevated a win-at-all-cost mentality to the fore in high school and youth sports. Winning has become such an overriding concern that many coaches find it hard to be character educators. And that means far too many coaches miss out on the endless procession of teachable moments that sports have to offer.

If we are going to transform the culture of youth sports to make it a positive, character-building experience for every youth athlete, we need to make the Double-Goal Coach the industry standard for every high school and youth coach. It's Double-Goal Coaches, after all, who are the kinds of coaches who are remembered by athletes as "difference makers" long after their playing days are over.

A Competitive Advantage

I am often surprised at how people misread me. Many people think I am a non-competitive person who just wants kids to have a good experience with sports. But the reality is somewhat different.

As I sometimes say when I speak about PCA, "I live in Northern California, and I like granola, but I am a very competitive person." I recognize that life is competitive (as well as cooperative) and that youth who don't learn to compete well will be at a competitive disadvantage in many arenas of life.

PCA is an organization of coaches and athletes who enjoy competing. We embrace competition as a way for coaches to teach important life lessons to youth, lessons that are perhaps better learned on the playing field than anywhere else.

As you'll see in the chapters ahead, being a Double-Goal Coach and achieving success on the field are not mutually exclusive. In fact, applying the principles of Double-Goal Coaching will actually give you a competitive advantage over win-at-all-cost coaching.

The Three Principles of Double-Goal Coaching

The Double-Goal Coach uses three main principles to prepare athletes to win on the scoreboard while teaching life lessons: The ELM Tree of Mastery, Filling Emotional Tanks, and Honoring the Game.

The ELM Tree of Mastery: Double-Goal Coaches share a goal with win-at-all-cost coaches – we want to win on the scoreboard. But we discipline ourselves to coach for mastery – focusing on getting better rather than focusing simply on winning – and recognize that winning is a by-product of moving athletes along the road to mastery of their sport.

The E in ELM stands for Effort, the L for Learning, and the M for bouncing back from Mistakes. When a coach focuses her players' attention on getting better and better, she gets better scoreboard results, as you will see in the next chapter. Coaching to the ELM Tree also has the benefit of providing youth with a framework that can help them be successful in whatever they choose to do in life beyond the playing field.

Filling Emotional Tanks: Everyone has an Emotional Tank like a car's gas tank. If your tank is empty, don't expect to go far. If your players' Emotional Tanks are empty, they are not going to perform at their best. Double-Goal Coaches discipline themselves to fill E-Tanks even when they are frustrated or angry because they know it will pay off in the long run. Chapter 5 goes into this in detail.

Honoring the Game: In a society in which civility and courtesy seem so often in short supply, it's crucial that Double-Goal Coaches model and teach Honoring the Game starting with ROOTS, which stands for respect for the **R**ules, **O**pponents, **O**fficials, **T**eammates, and **S**elf. Chapter 7 explores this crucial concept.

Double-Goal Coaches use these principles to coach in a more productive way than win-at-all-cost coaches. Chapters 4, 6, and 8 provide practical tools you can use to implement each principle with your teams.

Triple-Impact Competitors

Double-Goal Coaches produce Triple-Impact Competitors who make themselves, their teammates, and the game better. There is a parallel between the Double-Goal Coach model and the Triple-Impact Competitor model. Double-Goal Coaches:

- Coach for mastery and teach the power of the ELM Tree so their athletes become committed to pursuing mastery themselves.

- Fill Emotional Tanks and teach athletes to be E-Tank fillers who find ways to make their teammates better. Because leadership is making people around you better and more productive, Double-Goal Coaches help athletes become leaders.

- Model and teach Honoring the Game so, win or lose, their athletes compete in a way that makes their family, school, and community proud of them.

Athletes tend to focus most of their effort on making themselves better, so you can have a big impact by helping them make their teammates and the game better.

The Second-Goal Parent

Coaches have a crucial role to play in getting parents to support, rather than undercut, a positive sports culture. In PCA Sports Parent workshops, we ask parents whose job it is to win games. Despite often exhibiting sideline behavior to the contrary, they get it right away – it's the job of the players and the coaches. Sports parents have a much more important role to play – to help their children take from sports lessons that will help them become successful, contributing members of society.

We ask parents to be "Second-Goal Parents." Let athletes and coaches worry about the first goal of winning on the scoreboard. Parents should have a laser focus on the second goal of ensuring their children develop positive character traits from their experience with youth sports.

A Vision of Youth Sports

Imagine a world in which youth sports competitions bring out the best in people and everyone involved with a team – coaches, athletes, parents, fans – feel proud of their team, win or lose.

As Tim Flannery, Assistant Director for the National Federation of State High School Associations, notes: "Someday everyone will recognize the terms Double-Goal Coach, Triple-Impact Competitor, and Second-Goal Parent. When this day comes, all who participate in sport will be assured of a positive experience."

This book starts with you, the coach, the key person in this vision who, by becoming a Double-Goal Coach, can help make the vision a reality with your own teams.

CHAPTER THREE

Coaching to The ELM Tree of Mastery

The information in this chapter is compelling.

Based on years of sport psychology research, it provides a means of getting any athlete to improve, sometimes dramatically and rapidly. It is not controversial among sport psychology experts, but it will be surprising to many coaches.

Here's the bottom line: coaches who coach their athletes to pursue mastery get better results than coaches who coach to win on the scoreboard. Mastery simply means focusing on getting better rather than on trying to win on the scoreboard. To athletes and coaches focused on mastery, scoreboard victories come as a byproduct of the disciplined commitment to mastery.

During the 2000 Summer Olympics, Joan Duda of the University of Birmingham (UK) conducted research on athletes coached in a mastery environment (or what Duda refers to as a "task" focus) versus those coached in a traditional scoreboard environment with a primary emphasis on bottom-line results. She discovered a statistically significant difference in performance:

> Athletes coached to focus on mastery won significantly more Olympic medals than their counterparts whose focus was on winning medals.

As Professor Duda discovered in her research on the Sydney Olympics, if you learn to coach for mastery, you will win more and have a competitive advantage over coaches who continue to coach to the scoreboard.

The Pony in the Sports Psychology Lecture

I remember sitting in a sport psychology lecture in 1999 trying desperately to make sense of the tables of tiny numbers on the screen behind the speaker. Reminded of an old joke about an optimistic boy surrounded by horse manure, I kept thinking, "There must be a pony in here somewhere."

I took pages of notes but couldn't quite figure out the "so-what factor" for coaches and sports parents. This troubled me because I had just launched Positive Coaching Alliance, and I felt obligated to translate the powerful insights of sport psychology into practical tools that millions of coaches and sports parents – the vast majority of whom have no access to a sport psychology consultant – could use to get the best out of athletes.

While on a long run a few days later, it hit me. The key principle of sport psychology that was underpinning the complex lecture is that you get the best results when you focus on what you can control and block out the rest.

That's it. That is the secret of sport psychology: focus on what you can control and block out the rest.

Now this is a big idea, with implications far beyond the playing field. But what is controllable and what isn't in the lives of athletes? The biggest uncontrollable is the scoreboard outcome of a competition. You can't control who wins a game: the quality of your opposition, officials' calls, the weather, and injuries all affect the outcome. The list of uncontrollables is endless.

Then what are the crucial aspects of competition that you can control?

That question led to a formulation that has been a central idea of Double-Goal Coaching ever since – the ELM Tree of Mastery.

The ELM Tree of Mastery

The ELM Tree of Mastery is
E for Effort,
L for Learning and improvement, and
M for bouncing back from Mistakes.

What was buried in the initially mystifying sport psychology lecture were the three keys to success in sports (and life, for that matter).

Athletes on your team absolutely will be successful sooner or later if they

- routinely give their best effort
- have a Teachable Spirit and learn from everything that happens to them
- don't let mistakes (or fear of mistakes) stop them

Redefining Winning

Emphasizing the ELM Tree rather than the scoreboard leads to redefining "winning." Let's compare the scoreboard and mastery definitions of a winner.

Scoreboard Definition	Mastery Definition
Results	Effort
Comparison with others	Learning and improvement
Mistakes are not okay	Mistakes are okay

Let me explain why the E, the L and the M are crucial for optimal performance.

The ELM Tree focuses on how hard you work while the larger culture is obsessed with scoreboard results. But focusing on the scoreboard is risky for many reasons. Your opponent may be extremely weak (or strong). You may have a run of very bad or good luck. On the other hand, focusing on effort will pay off in every situation.

Implicit in the ELM Tree is that comparisons with others are not helpful. A better comparison is with oneself. Am I better now than I was at the beginning of the season? Will I be better at the end of the season than I am now? If so, you are a winner, regardless of the temporary results on the scoreboard because these are questions designed to lead to improvement. They also keep each player motivated to learn, even ones who are on teams with much weaker players.

Finally, mistakes are inevitable. When we ask our players to give 100 percent and to try to learn new things, they are bound to make mistakes. And if you think about it, it is much better that they make mistakes than to stop extending themselves because they are afraid of making a mistake.

The Power (and Paradox) of the ELM Tree

Much research supports the ELM Tree of Mastery, but let me put it simply.

1 **ELM = Control:** Athletes can't control the outcome of a competition. But they absolutely can learn to control all elements of the ELM Tree: a) their level of effort, b) whether they learn from their experience, and c) how they respond to the inevitable mistakes they will make. Internalizing the ELM Tree makes athletes feel more in control of their own destiny.

2 **Anxiety:** When athletes feel in control, their anxiety decreases which frees up nervous energy for accomplishing a task rather than worrying about failing.

3 **Self-Confidence:** Self-confidence also increases when athletes feel in control. And when self-confidence increases, athletes tend to work harder and stick to it longer as research by Stanford's Albert Bandura has demonstrated. This is a huge idea so I am going to repeat it: if you increase an athlete's self-confidence, he will work harder and stick to a task longer.

That's the power of the ELM Tree. The paradox is that by focusing on mastery, athletes actually do better on the scoreboard. You win more by not focusing on winning! Scoreboard wins come as a by-product of a relentless pursuit of mastery.

Athletes are more likely to internalize the ELM Tree if they have coaches who emphasize the virtues of mastery and de-emphasize results on the scoreboard. This, in turn, helps them feel in control, experience decreased anxiety, and feel more self-confident, so they can perform better.

Recent research by University of Washington researchers Ronald Smith, Frank Smoll, and Sean Cumming demonstrates another important advantage of a mastery environment. When coaches create a mastery climate, their athletes enjoy their sport more as the season progresses – and they tend to keep doing things they enjoy.

I have always felt that the test of a good youth coach is whether his or her players return the next season. There are so many benefits to youth who stick with sports that coaches have not been successful even if they win a championship if their players end up dropping out. Ronald Smith: "One consistent finding of our research is that a mastery climate retains more youngsters in sports. It keeps them coming back."

Avoiding the Talent Trap

Carol Dweck of Stanford University, author of *Mindset: The New Psychology of Success,* has identified two different "mindsets" that possess enormous implications for coaches and link directly to the ELM Tree of Mastery concept.

The first is the "Fixed Mindset," in which an athlete sees ability as set. Either you have talent or you don't. Either you are smart or you aren't. This mindset is a dead-end because whether you succeed or not is determined by something totally outside your control.

The other is the "Growth Mindset." You believe in your ability to grow and improve, regardless of where you start. This is a wonderful thought for any young person: "I can get smarter (or better at learning a foreign language or excelling in a sport or…) if I work hard at it."

Dweck's idea is especially important for youth athletes who must make and react to countless mistakes as they learn a sport. As Dweck states, "People with a fixed mindset think effort is for people without talent. They are afraid of making mistakes so they hide them. Learning takes a back seat to looking good...It's in the growth mindset where people believe that you can develop talent – it's not fixed – that the whole idea of effort, learning, and confronting mistakes is inherent in the framework."

On the flip side, if an athlete does something well, either on the playing field or off, Dweck's research offers clear guidance on the appropriate type of feedback coaches should give to avoid the talent trap.

Wrong: For example, a coach might say, *"Wow, that was a great play. You've got talent!"* This focus on talent reinforces the Fixed Mindset and the idea that the child has little or no control over his development. A tough challenge in the future then becomes even tougher because talented people aren't supposed to be stumped by a challenge.

Right: On the other hand, you could say, *"Wow, that was a great play. You've really been working hard, and it's paying off!"* This reinforces the Growth Mindset that good play is a result of effort, which will more likely cause her to try harder in the future when faced with a challenge that initially stymies her.

Because many athletes believe ability is independent of effort and beyond their control, Dweck argues that it is crucial to introduce and reinforce the Growth Mindset to prepare the way for the ELM Tree.

And research indicates that you and your athletes will be glad if you do. Dr. Dweck again: "We did a study of college athletes looking at whether they believed their coaches valued effort and practice or natural talent and outcomes. The more they believed their coaches valued effort and practice, the better they did that year and the more they improved."

In the next chapter, we'll share some practical tools to bring the ELM Tree of Mastery to life for your athletes.

CHAPTER FOUR

The ELM Tree of Mastery Toolkit

Resiliency is a key success factor for athletes. Without it, athletes, no matter how talented, are just not going to be successful. Over the course of a season (or a career), athletes must weather storms in the form of injuries, upset defeats, slumps, and illness.

Joan Duda, whose research was highlighted in Chapter 3, says: "Everyone looks at the scoreboard. But you have to have other criteria besides the scoreboard – it is not one or the other. What's different about athletes who are primarily task-oriented is that they have other ways to keep the boat afloat when things don't tilt in their direction. The magic of a task focus is the resiliency it provides us…it's the mortar that holds the bricks together, especially when under attack."

A mastery orientation (Duda's "task" focus) helps athletes deal with the inevitable difficult situations they will face. The practical tools in this chapter can help players develop a mastery orientation to serve them throughout their lives.

1 | "Plant and Water" the ELM Tree

Before athletes can internalize the ELM Tree of Mastery, they need to hear it and talk about it, a lot. Help them by planting the seeds early in the season. Jot down some talking points to share with them. For example:

- The Tree of Mastery is an ELM Tree. ELM stands for E for Effort, L for Learning, M for bouncing back from Mistakes.

- Research shows athletes who focus on ELM improve faster and do better on the scoreboard. To be our best, we should focus on ELM.

- If you give your best effort, I'll be proud of you no matter what the score is.

- Learning requires having a Teachable Spirit. Let's try to learn something to get better every day.

- Great competitors don't throw a tantrum when they make a mistake; they reset on the next play and later try to learn from their mistake.

- I want you to play with enthusiasm and be aggressive. It's okay to make a mistake – the key is to bounce back quickly so you can make the next play.

Once planted, the ELM Tree requires constant watering because the larger sports culture constantly undermines a mastery focus. Media coverage of professional sports focuses almost exclusively on scoreboard winners, ignores great efforts that come up short, shows disdain for those who don't win, and says in so many ways that the only thing ultimately that matters is winning on the scoreboard. Here are some ways to keep the ELM Tree growing despite the larger sports culture.

- Discuss the ELM Tree during practices and games. Recognize players working hard, learning something new, and bouncing back from mistakes, and use the occasion to reinforce the ELM Tree. Reinforce a Growth Mindset by focusing on their effort whenever they do something right: "Your defense was much improved on Saturday. I see all your hard work is paying off."

- Before every game, remind your players they will perform better if they focus on the ELM Tree.

- Give your players a "homework" assignment to watch their sport at the college or professional level on television and write down at least one thing they learned that they could try in their own practice.

- Share your commitment to mastery. Talk about books you read, videos you watch, clinics you attend, and the time you expend in planning practices. If you also talk about how you use the ELM Tree in your regular life, you will help your players think about the ELM Tree in their life outside sports.

2 | Help Players Recover Quickly with a Mistake Ritual

Mistakes are what youth athletes worry about most. Once a player makes a mistake in public (and the playing field, even with few spectators, is very public for youth athletes), they are no longer in the moment. Negative self-talk kicks in, they berate themselves silently for making a mistake, and are usually not ready for the next play.

A mistake ritual is a gesture and statement that coaches and players use to transform the fear of mistakes so they don't play timidly. A mistake ritual allows athletes to quickly "reset" for the next play without beating themselves up for having made a mistake. Here are a few examples Double-Goal Coaches have used successfully:

- The Flush: Motion like you're flushing a toilet. "It's okay, Omar. Flush it. Next play."

- No Sweat: Wipe two fingers across your forehead as if flicking sweat from your brow. "No sweat. Forget it. Get ready for the next play!"

- Brush It Off: Motion as if brushing dirt off your shoulder while yelling, "Brush it off."

Encourage your team to not fear mistakes and discuss what mistake ritual they'd like to use. Urge players to use it with each other whenever a mistake is made.

The power of a Mistake Ritual is well documented. The "flush" helped Louisiana State University win the 2009 NCAA baseball title!

- Ryan Schimpf after hitting a home run in the Super Regional to beat Rice: "I had two terrible at-bats previously, and I just tried to flush it."

- Pitcher Anthony Ranaudo after a bad outing against Virginia: "I just have to be able to flush it mentally and go out there with a new attitude and approach." He then pitched 6 shutout innings to defeat Arkansas in the College World Series.

- LSU Head Coach Paul Mainieri after losing to Texas in the tournament: "This just wasn't our night. We have to flush this loss and come out ready to play for the national championship on Wednesday night" – which they won. And the pitcher who picked up the win in the final game? Frequent flusher Anthony Ranaudo.

Baseball lends itself to mistake rituals, but the tool works in any sport. As a college hockey goalie, PCA's Eric Eisendrath brushed snow away from the posts after goals scored against him to create a mental "clean slate." One youth soccer coach has players pretend to be holding a balloon by a string, and simply let it go by opening their clenched fist.

While we don't want kids to fear mistakes, we also recognize they shouldn't be ignored. It is the coach's responsibility to correct mistakes. That's why having a "Parking Lot" is helpful.

Correcting mistakes immediately after they're made is often not pragmatic (like in the midst of a fast-paced game). Further, the moment after a mistake is not a teachable moment for most youth athletes.

Instead, note the mistake without mentioning it at the time, and "park" it where you will remember it after the game so you can address it. (Chapter 6 offers tips for giving constructive feedback effectively.)

Later you can try to understand why the athlete made the mistake so you can help her improve. Maybe she was never taught the skill adequately. Or maybe she didn't understand what you asked her to do. Maybe the skill is a complex one and, although she understands what you want her to do, she hasn't mastered it physically.

Often, a player can perform an action until fatigued, which opens the floodgates for mistakes late in competitions. Sometimes nervousness causes a player to not execute something he can do easily in practice. Rarely does a player understand what you have asked him to do and intentionally disregard your wishes, although this may happen once in a blue moon. Whatever the reason for the mistake, using a mistake ritual and the Parking Lot helps you get the best from your players.

3 | Make Effort Goals a Part of Your Team Culture

Double-Goal Coaches tap into the enormous power of Effort Goals, which are more under a player's control than outcome goals. Effort Goals motivate because players can control their effort and see their progress. Here are some examples of Effort Goals:

	Effort Goals	Outcome Goals
Baseball/ Softball	· Run hard through first base on a grounder	· Beat the throw to first
Basketball	· Make contact and block out after every shot	· Get the rebound
Lacrosse	· Contest every ground ball	· Gain possession of the ball
Soccer	· Sprint after all 50-50 balls	· Get to the ball first and control it
Football	· Relentlessly pursue the ball until you hear the whistle	· Make the tackle

Effort Goals are great for younger kids and those new to a sport or less skilled. With a timid beginning soccer player, you might set an effort goal for her to contest every ball within 10 feet and get at least five touches in a half. Ask a less skilled basketball player to race back on defense each time and quickly find the person he's guarding.

Effort Goals also work well with older, more seasoned athletes. To get my high school basketball team to drive to the basket, we set an Effort Goal of shooting at least 20 free throws per game. Taking the ball aggressively to the basket often led opponents to foul, putting my players on the line. If we achieved our Effort Goal of 20 free throws in the game, we usually also achieved our outcome goal of winning the game.

Effort Goals that "move the goal posts" can keep teams trying throughout a game or season regardless of the score. My friend Wayne Pinegar once coached a team of U-9 girls in a challenging soccer season. In the opening minutes of the first game his team scored what turned out to be their only goal of the season.

Wayne developed a set of Effort Goals to keep the team from getting discouraged because they had virtually no chance of winning on the scoreboard. One was to move the ball past the mid-line at least five times in a game.

Well behind near the end of the final game, his players and parents on the sidelines suddenly cheered loudly. Their celebration confused the opposing team and parents – why was the losing team celebrating? The answer, of course, was that it was the fifth time they moved the ball past midfield. When a coach uses Effort Goals, players feel good about their improvement and can continue giving best efforts even when losing by a big margin on the scoreboard. As a postscript, every girl on Wayne's team came out for soccer again the next year, an amazing accomplishment in a zero-win season.

Effort Goals are also useful for talented teams when winning easily. If a team has put the game away early, have players focus on using weak hands or feet, trying a move that they have not yet mastered, or playing new positions. This way Effort Goals challenge a talented team even during runaway victories.

Effort Goals are even more powerful when players set their own. You can "seed" the discussion by suggesting some Effort Goals and asking players to select the ones they'd like to achieve. Have them share their goals with you, their teammates, and/or parents to strengthen their commitment to achieving them.

4 | Improve Performance with Stretch Goals

Stretch Goals improve performance. A Stretch Goal is something you can't do right away, so a stretch is required. Stretch Goals go a little beyond what people think they can do, but are reachable with effort over time. Here are some examples:

- *Basketball:* Improve three-point shot percentage to 40 percent
- *Soccer:* Increase distance of a goal-kick by 10 yards
- *Swimming:* Improve start and turns to drop 5 seconds off 100 freestyle time
- *Lacrosse:* Cradle the ball with weak hand high as skillfully as with strong hand
- *Baseball:* Hit outside pitches to the opposite field consistently
- *Football:* Regularly make catches just with hands, not the body

Here's why Stretch Goals work: if we set an ambitious goal, we know instinctively we can't achieve it the old way. We have to try something new or work harder (or both). A Stretch Goal can be a catalyst to learning what it takes to do what we want to do.

The ideal Stretch Goal can become a "Just-Right Challenge," in which athletes are excited to take on a challenge because it feels within reach with some extra effort. When athletes (or anyone) are facing a Just-Right Challenge, motivation is a non-issue. They can't wait to tackle it.

Ask athletes to think of Stretch Goals that are Just-Right Challenges for them. Help them develop a practical, step-by-step plan to achieve them. Have them revisit their Stretch Goals regularly to ensure they aren't discouragingly hard (or boringly easy). Help them adjust goals to be more achievable and motivating, or set new goals when achieved. As with Effort Goals, Stretch Goals are most powerful when players set their own.

Teams can set Stretch Goals as well. When I coached high school girls' basketball, my captains decided to shoot for the Central Coast Section (California) title in our division.

I worried that this goal was too ambitious and almost suggested focusing on winning our league title. But I didn't discourage them from their stretch goal, and we won our league. I believe part of our success was that we set our sights high. If we had set only the lower goal of winning our league, we might well have fallen short of that. The higher, more unrealistic goal actually was more practical.

5 | Maximize Effort By Rewarding Unsuccessful Effort

All coaches reward players who make the play. It sounds crazy, but to maximize team effort, reward players who try hard but *fail* to make the play.

When a player makes the play and is cheered by her coach, she will tend to assume her coach is happy about the outcome, even if the coach stresses the effort involved. So look for great efforts that aren't successful. Then when you praise a player's effort, there is no confusion. You can only be recognizing the player for effort, which sends a message that you notice effort no matter what the outcome.

This tool can transform your own negativity when a player fails to make a play. A coach who understands the power of this tool for building a team of gritty, relentless players will be less disappointed at failure because he will see it as an ideal teachable moment to strengthen his team's habit of effort.

PCA's Tina Syer notes that in field hockey and soccer, wings who stay wide force defenders to cover them, which can leave the striker open. Sometimes a player will run 60 yards down field but not be rewarded with the ball. Tina makes sure to recognize this so they will make this long run to be in the right place in the future. In the absence of recognition, a player may not do this again, especially since it is hard work.

Mike Legarza wanted his college basketball players to drive to the basket aggressively, so he never criticized them for missing a lay-up. I once saw him react to a missed lay-up with, "Great drive, John!" He overlooked the failure to reward the unsuccessful effort.

Opportunities to reinforce unsuccessful effort abound in every sport.

6 | Get Things Done with Targeted Symbolic Rewards

What gets rewarded gets done. What the coach gives attention to gets done because a coach's attention is rewarding to players. Targeted Symbolic Rewards can get athletes to act in helpful ways without undercutting internal motivation, which can happen with external rewards.

After games, recognize players who worked hard or completed unsung activities such as marking opponents on defense or hustling after loose balls. Make sure the reward is "symbolic" (not something of value in and of itself). Here are some examples:

- John Buxton, Headmaster at Culver Academies (IN), gives lollypops to players who do something he wants to see more of, especially effort. He occasionally gives lollypops to players who star in conventional ways (e.g., hitting a home run), but mostly he targets unsung activities that contribute to the team's success. "Sam, you backed up third on that triple in the fifth inning. That's the kind of thinking and hustle we need." Lollypops make post-game conversations something players look forward to.

- Greg Siino, a Roseville (CA) coach, uses the transcontinental railroad to reinforce unsung behavior with "The Golden Spike Award." He has players visualize a cross-country train ride in which spikes typically go unnoticed, but the train would derail without them holding the rails in place. He gives the award to someone who does something to build the team or support a teammate. He especially looks for players who react maturely to a bad call, who rise above a bad game to help the team, or who do something positive when tired at the end of a game or during conditioning.

- Lisa Christiansen, a coach for the U-19 U.S. world champion women's lacrosse team, awards a special blue ball at the first practice of the week to the athlete who worked the hardest the previous week, used a new skill successfully in the game or, when it's rainy, came off the field the muddiest. That athlete gets to use the blue ball all week during drills at the start of practice. This became such a big deal to her players that they won't allow Christiansen to start practice until she announces the winner for that week.

- Some coaches give out a "Dirty Shirt Award" after each game to the player who shows the grittiest play. Others allow players who showed exemplary hustle or bounced back from a mistake to pick the music for the next practice or wear special practice jerseys that week.

Whatever behavior you want to see more of, create a symbolic reward for it, and you will!

5

CHAPTER FIVE

The Athlete's Emotional Tank

A pervasive image from professional sports on television is a coach yelling at a player who failed to make a play or do what the coach wanted. While this is often regarded as toughness on the part of the coach, I think it generally is a lack of discipline that undermines a coach's ability to get the best from players.

Each person has an "Emotional Tank" like the gas tank in a car. If your gas tank is empty, you are not going to go very far no matter how wonderful your car is.

The Portable Home Team Advantage

Coaches who yell and demean players drain their Emotional Tanks. And none of us does our best with drained E-Tanks. When E-Tanks are low, athletes tend to be pessimistic, give up more easily, and become defensive in the face of criticism. An athlete with a drained E-Tank likely will not perform as well as that same athlete with an overflowing E-Tank.

When Emotional Tanks are full, players are more coachable, they tend to be optimistic, and they deal better with adversity. Coaches who regularly fill their players' E-Tanks provide their team with the equivalent of a portable home team advantage. It's as if they played all their games at home in front of a huge supportive crowd that thinks they can do no wrong.

We all could use one or more Emotional Tank fillers in our lives. Having someone who provides unconditional support and truthful and specific praise encourages us and improves performance and attitude.

Learn to fill your players' Emotional Tanks and you will develop the equivalent of a portable home team advantage. Your players will be more enthusiastic and harder working. And it will help you on the scoreboard, because it's no accident that the home team wins almost 60 percent of the time in college and professional sports.

Filling and Draining Your Players' Emotional Tank

The Emotional Tank is not rocket science. Here are ways to fill your players' tanks:

Tank Fillers	Examples
Truthful, specific praise	"Nice effort! You hustled and fought for all four quarters." "I loved the way you kept your eye on the ball and followed through."
Express appreciation	"It was great the way you pumped up your teammates before we made our comeback." "Thanks for helping pick up the balls."
Listening	"How else do you think we can attack their zone defense?" "How do you think practice went today?"
Nonverbal actions	Smiling, clapping, nodding, thumbs up

Praise is a tank-filler when truthful and specific. Rather than a generic "Good job," say, "I really appreciated the way you gave 100 percent. Even in a losing effort, you ran out every ground ball, got into good defensive position before every pitch, and pulled for your teammates in the dugout. I can't ask for more."

Be careful not to praise when unwarranted. Instead, be on the lookout for specific and positive things to say to your athletes. Kids can sniff out empty approval.

Listening is one of the most powerful tank fillers. Ask your athletes what they think about practices and games. Ask them about favorite movies, summer plans, and hobbies. It's been said, "People don't care what you know unless they know you care." Listening shows you care.

While we all need refreshers in tank filling, most of us are pretty natural tank drainers. We often find it easier to see what is wrong and comment on it than to reinforce laudable behavior. Here are common tank drainers:

Tank Drainers	Examples
Criticize and correct	"You should have gotten more loose balls. Be more aggressive, like Maria."
	"That swing was weak. Come on. Get with it."
Sarcasm	"What were you thinking on that play?"
	"SpongeBob can kick the ball harder than that!"
Ignoring	"Not now."
	"Maybe later."
Nonverbal	Frowning, eye-rolling, heavy sighing

The Magic Ratio

Research shows that the optimal ratio of tank-fillers to criticisms is 5 to 1. University of Washington Professor John Gottman calls this the Magic Ratio. I love that name because you do see magical things happen as you get close to 5:1.

Gottman found marriages at the 5:1 level tended to last, while divorces were more likely at lower ratios. Research in the classroom by Robert and Evelyn Kirkhart also showed a 5:1 ratio to be ideal for stimulating children's learning. When the ratio dropped to 2:1 or lower, they found children's attitude became one of despair.

As coach of the Chicago Bulls, Phil Jackson embraced the Magic Ratio concept in his coaching of Horace Grant. Jackson would regularly yell at Grant, with Horace's permission, as a way to motivate the rest of the team. Over time, Jackson came to see he was de-motivating Grant, as he described in a talk he gave to PCA in March 2001.

"We had a falling out…Horace and I had to reach a new territory. About that time, Jim's book shows up, and Positive Coaching becomes an influence in my life, the 5:1 ratio, five praises to one critique. Well, Horace and I were going about 1:3 at that time (laughter), so I made a reasonable effort to get to 2:1. I couldn't possibly get to 5:1 because, after all, these are pros, and they are expected to perform with some excellence. But we did get to 2:1, and Horace and I had a wonderful relationship, and, of course, the rest we know is that these Bulls won three championships in a row. And it was great."

Keep track of your "plus/minus" ratio for a while to see what your baseline is. Then work to get it up to the 5:1 level and enjoy the "magic."

In the next chapter, we'll share some practical tools for making tank-filling an integral part of your team's culture.

The E-Tank in Life

Daniel Goleman has written extensively about the power of "emotional intelligence," the ability to recognize emotions in oneself and others, and manage one's feelings so as to be able to motivate oneself and handle relationships with others. He says that, all things equal, emotional intelligence may be more important than conventional intelligence or IQ. If two individuals have the same IQ, the one with more emotional intelligence is likely to be more successful.

How can you equip your athletes to increase their emotional intelligence? Start by teaching them about the Emotional Tank and how to fill it. You will be giving them a concept that will help them be successful throughout their lives at the same time you build them into a team that will have more success on the scoreboard.

CHAPTER SIX

The Emotional Tank Toolkit

Individuals who fill other people's Emotional Tanks will be successful in life. People want to work for and with E-Tank fillers. The tools in this chapter are designed to make you a great tank-filling coach as well as a developer of Triple-Impact Competitors who develop leadership skills and make their teammates better.

1 | Model and Teach the Importance of Filling Emotional Tanks

Be a frequent filler of Emotional Tanks. Every practice and every game, find things you can use to fill your players' E-Tanks. Model tank-filling so your players will be more inclined to becoming tank fillers themselves.

Jot down some simple talking points to use with your players at the first practice and then come back to them regularly. For example:

• We all have Emotional Tanks.

• E-Tanks are like gas tanks in cars; to go far you need a full tank.

• People perform better with full E-Tanks, so let's learn to fill each other's tanks.

• Thanking people and noticing when they do well fills E-Tanks.

• Helping your teammates bounce back from a mistake also fills E-Tanks.

• If we all become tank fillers, we'll have more fun and be a better team.

2 | Use the Buddy System to Make Your Players Tank-Fillers

Get your players filling each other's E-tanks, and your team will go far. Introduce the Buddy System early in the season and use it at least two to three times a week.

Pair up players. Make sure you don't pick the same pairs each time – you want everyone to get used to filling everyone's tank. "You have two jobs here. Do the drill as well as you can and look for ways to fill your partner's E-Tank."

Right after the drill, ask your players who got their tank filled by their partners. At this point you may get blank stares if they forgot about tank filling as they concentrated on the drill. That's okay, because it's not what you teach, it's what you emphasize. You have your players for an entire season, so you can emphasize tank-filling again and again. If you get blank stares, you may want to do the same drill over again right away. This time tell your players to make sure they focus on filling their partner's tank.

Teams whose members learn to fill each other's E-Tanks not only have great seasons, they tend to perform better as the season progresses.

3 | Develop Player-Coaches

A sports team is a great place to develop leaders, and individuals become leaders by learning how to make decisions. Coaches who treat their players like trained monkeys and tell them what to do all the time are doing them a disservice. Here are two ways to develop players as leaders who function as player-coaches.

- **Ask rather than tell.** Get in the habit of asking rather than telling players what to do next. "Okay, if they line up in the shotgun, how should we adjust our defense?" This forces them to think and learn rather than wait for you to tell them what to do. It also is great to ask rather than tell after a mistake. "If you are in the same situation next time, what can you do differently?"

- **Ask for input.** When you ask your players for input into your decisions, you fill their E-Tanks and you get them to think. And it can start really simply. "We're going to do these three drills today. Which makes the most sense to start with?"

Notice here you didn't give up any real control. You will still do the same drills, but you have now involved them in the decision-making. This can also work in much more crucial situations where you do actually share control with your players.

Ernie Dossa, who I coached against when I was at Fremont High School, involved his Homestead High players in a key decision when they played a more talented team for the Central Coast Section championship. He asked his players which of three defensive schemes they wanted to use for the big game. They picked an unusual 3-2 zone designed to keep the other team's 3-point shooters covered. I believe they won the game and the championship partly because the players felt more engaged and committed to making their choice work.

4 | Inject Positive Energy with the Two-Minute Drill

I am always amazed at how the energy levels of pro football players pick up at the end of a game when they run their two-minute drill needing a score to win. They know there is only a little time left so they are less likely to hold anything back.

You can do your own Two-Minute Drill whenever the energy level in a practice or game gets low. Pick a time period (an inning, a specific drill, the last 5 minutes of a period) and amp up your positivity level. Look for anything you can be positive about and then comment on it energetically. "Courtney, great hustle! Silvia, nice move! Emily, I like that, keep it up! Lindsay, you showed me something just now!"

This is a time when you intentionally do not critique anyone or anything. Correct mistakes another time. Right now you are giving your players an infusion of positive energy, and you don't want anything to get in the way of it.

Former Stanford Women's Tennis Coach Frank Brennan, winner of 10 NCAA titles, shared with me his version of the Two-Minute Drill, which he often used on low-energy Mondays. He'd start at Court 1 and watch until he saw something from each player he could be positive about. He'd comment and move to Court 2, where he did the same. By the time he'd made his way to the last court, it seemed like a totally different team. Everyone was pumped up by his injection of positive energy.

5 | Turn Kids Around with Player of the Day

If we are honest, we will admit that we all have had players that we didn't relate well to. Some kids just push our buttons. When you have a player like this, make him Player of the Day. Don't tell the player this, but make sure to get your co-coaches on the same page. "Today, Colin is Player of the Day. Every time he does anything the least bit positive, we reinforce him for it."

If he runs hard for half a drill, say, "Colin, great hustle at the beginning!" All your attention goes to things he is doing well. Ignore the things he is not doing well.

This tool can make a huge difference with kids who regularly have empty E-Tanks. Many kids have problems at home, in school, or with friends, and they come to your practice with a chip on their shoulder. When you make a player like this Player of the Day, you do two important things.

You fill his tank in a way he is not used to and which he cannot ignore. Even for disturbed, behavior-problem kids (and I have worked extensively with them), this kind of tank filling makes them feel better about themselves.

The other thing that happens is that you begin to see the player in a better light. Cognitive dissonance happens when our behavior and our thoughts are not aligned, and that is uncomfortable. We don't like acting in ways that are different from our feelings and thoughts, so we change one or the other. When you treat Colin as Player of the Day, your attitude toward him becomes more positive as well. And having a coach who becomes more positive toward him is a very good thing for Colin!

6 | Vary the Pace with Fun

Excelling in a sport is a fine balance of fun and hard work. If it becomes too much of either one, it loses some of its power. Make sure you incorporate fun activities into your practices on a regular basis.

PCA's Tina Syer uses the "Shadow Game" with her elite field hockey players, but it works just as well with younger kids. Players pair up with the person who is trying to step on the shadow of the other player who, of course, is trying to keep her from doing just that. Tina's players worked so hard at this game, which they loved, it helped them keep in shape as well as filled their E-Tanks.

You can inject fun into practice by manipulating the degree of difficulty. I had my teen baseball players play tee-ball, and they loved literally teeing off on the ball. Increase the difficulty in soccer by requiring players to only pass or shoot with their weaker foot. Tennis matches in which only one square on either side of the net is "in" are a blast and help develop a short game. Play "Work Up" in baseball or softball with two or three players on a team. One team is at bat with all the other teams in the field. The team at bat has to bring the final player home (to bat again) or that player is out. After three outs, the next team bats, and so forth.

Competition almost always increases the fun for athletes. A paired shooting drill with the loser doing a push-up creates some intensity and excitement in what otherwise might be a pretty routine drill. Even better is a competition between players and coaches, with the coaches doing the push-up if they lose (and savvy coaches lose occasionally!).

If you don't know what your players will think is fun, ask them. Let them pick or even design activities they will have fun with. Fun activities typically get players laughing and fill them with energy that carries into the rest of your practice.

7 | Use Positive Charting to Get More of the Behavior You Want

Every time I have used Positive Charting it has paid big dividends, but it requires some planning and a commitment to follow through.

Put a sheet of paper on a clipboard with each player's name and space below for notes for each. (You can make your own form or get a copy from the PCA web site – see page 70.) Put a box labeled "Look-For" next to each name.

During the game, write positive things a player does – the more specific, the better. Make sure you have about the same number of good things for each player. It's easy to note many positive things for talented players and often hard to find anything for weaker players. For talented players, note the difficult things they are doing. For the weaker players, look hard, and you'll find some things you can be positive about. Be disciplined. At the end of the game you want two to five items for each player.

If there is a specific behavior a player is working on (e.g., blocking out for rebounds, hitting the hole quickly, or staying wide on attack) put that in the Look-For Box. Before the game let him know what you will be looking for from him in the game. Remember to look for team-building things like E-Tank filling as well as physical actions.

This is a great tool for involving assistant coaches, parents, and players who are sitting on the bench if you are careful to train them to follow the above procedure. It will help them see the game in a new way.

I used Positive Charting to turn around a horrible beginning to my second season coaching high school basketball, which I describe in my book *Shooting in the Dark*. Here is the experience of a softball coach from Ohio with Positive Charting.

"At the beginning of the season, the only team these girls could beat was themselves…Well, after one mediocre game, I sat the girls down on the bench and instead of reading them the riot act…I mentioned all the positive aspects of the game they played just to show these girls that they were capable of doing some positive things. I did this after each game from then on, win or lose. Wouldn't you know it, these same rag tag girls lost the last game of the season: the city championship game by one run (to a team that annihilated them by 12 runs in the first game of that season.)"

Positive Charting can seem like magic. If you try it, you won't regret it. Begin each practice with a quick team conversation taking 30 seconds to spotlight each player in turn. Then enjoy the positive energy of your players during the practice!

8 | Give Receivable Feedback with Kid-Friendly Criticism

Criticism and correction are important to learning, but they often drain people's tanks, which decreases their capacity to learn. John Robinson, who as football coach at the University of Southern California won a national championship, understood the tank-draining impact of criticism. I love his statement: "I never criticize players until they are first convinced of my unconditional confidence in their abilities."

Kid-Friendly Criticism provides players with useable information that empowers them to improve while minimizing tank draining. Here are some practical ways to give players Kid-Friendly Criticism:

- **Avoid non-teachable moments.** There is too much emotion in some moments for criticism to be heard or acted upon, no matter how accurate, well-meaning, and perfectly delivered it may be. Discipline yourself after a tough loss or a painful mistake. Wait until the emotion has dissipated before giving feedback.

- **Criticize in private.** Anyone can be embarrassed by public criticism, so wait until you can give a player feedback in private. Praise in public; criticize in private.

- **Ask permission.** Asking permission makes criticism easier to hear and apply, especially for the kind of youth who may not be able to handle feedback. "Judy, I noticed something that might improve your shooting. Are you open to hearing it?" If she says, "No," honor that and return to it later. Her curiosity may even cause her to come to ask you about it. But don't use this tool for something that requires immediate intervention, such as poor sportsmanship or safety.

- **Use If-Then statements.** If-Then statements are easier for kids to hear than telling them what to do. "If you bend your knees when you shoot, then you'll get better range on your 3-point shots" works better than saying, "Bend your knees when you shoot," especially if done in an annoyed tone of voice. If-Then statements help players feel in control, which makes them more open to criticism.

- **Give them a criticism sandwich.** Sandwich a criticism or correction between two positive reinforcements. "I like the way you keep your eyes on the basket when you shoot. If you bend your knees more, you'll get better range. And nice follow through!" You've just given three pieces of feedback and made the criticism easier to take.

9 | End Games with Winner's Circle

The end of a game is a crucial time for a team because of the emotion generated by a competition. Right after a game is ideal for focusing on tank filling using a Winner's Circle. Get your players into a circle and open the floor for tank-filling comments. "Who noticed someone doing something to help our team today?"

Generally, it works best if you speak last. However, you can also seed your comments in between players' comments. You can highlight unsung actions or great efforts while also keeping an eye on who is not getting any tank filling so you can mention their contributions.

No matter how poorly your team played, end with a positive. It's a coach's job to motivate players, especially after a tough loss, so find something positive to say to your players to get them to come to the next practice ready to work hard and improve. Your next practice actually starts with the last thing you say to your team after a game, so find something they did that gives hope for improvement.

CHAPTER SEVEN

Beyond Sportsmanship: Honoring the Game

Rarely does a week go by that I don't hear one or more examples of egregious behavior on the part of youth coaches and parents (rarely youth athletes who pretty much behave themselves until they approach adulthood). Some parents in particular seem to operate on hair-triggers whenever they perceive their child being treated less than fairly. But coaches also often fail to live up to their responsibility as role models and shapers of young people.

At the same time, our larger culture seems to be degrading into one in which a win-at-all-cost attitude prevails. Civility is becoming a scarce commodity, with public figures and ordinary people acting in ways that degrade the social conversation with no apparent remorse.

I am convinced there is a connection between the two. What happens in the larger society affects how coaches and parents interact in youth sports, and the experiences people have with youth sports in turn have an impact on the larger society. I agree with Thomas Boswell who said that sport has become "the meeting ground where we discuss our values" in this extremely diverse society.

This brings me to you as a positive change agent. As a youth coach, you can go with the flow and accelerate the degradation, or you can go against the grain and help to reverse the degradation by modeling and teaching your athletes and their families to Honor the Game.

A Crucial Mistake

At Positive Coaching Alliance, we define culture as "the way we do things here." The underlying problem is that youth sports has slid into the professional sports way of doing things.

Professional sports is an entertainment business with the goal all businesses have of making a profit. This requires entertaining fans, which in turn usually requires a winning team. Thus at the professional level, a win-at-all-cost mentality too often prevails. And because winning seems so important, pro sports fans tend to see their role as doing whatever they can to help "their" team win.

Because youth sports resembles professional sports – in rules, equipment, strategy – many people make the crucial mistake of thinking the two are the same. But pro sports and youth sports are fundamentally different enterprises. Youth sports is about developing young men and women into great people who contribute to their society and achieve success in their careers and family lives.

That means that youth coaches need to behave in an appreciably different way from coaches and athletes involved in professional sports.

The ROOTS of Honoring the Game

Honoring the Game is a more robust version of sportsmanship. Unfortunately, sportsmanship has lost much of its power to inspire and now seems like a list of don't-do's – "Don't yell at officials" or "Don't throw your helmet." Honoring the Game is a concept to inspire and motivate people to live up to their best, rather than simply to be restricted from acting down to their worst.

If we want family members who help each other achieve their dreams, neighbors who are friendly and pitch in, business owners who pursue profit ethically, people from different traditions and backgrounds who respect one another – in short, if we want everyday decency in our society – then we can begin by teaching our youth how to compete in sports with grace and humility.

The ROOTS of Honoring the Game describe the behavior we want to teach and model, where ROOTS represents respect for: **Rules, Opponents, Officials, Teammates,** and **Self.**

Rules: We want to win the way the game is supposed to be played. We refuse to bend the rules even when we can get away with it, whether anyone is looking or not. Rules have been developed and carefully modified to make games as fair as possible. Breaking them undercuts fairness.

No rulebook can cover every situation. There will always be ambiguity that the rules simply don't address. Crafty individuals can find ways to circumvent the exact wording of any rule. People who Honor the Game respect both the spirit and the letter of the rules.

Opponents: A worthy opponent is a gift. Imagine a tug-of-war with no one at the other end of the rope. Without opponents, competitive sports make no sense. It's also not much fun to beat up on a much weaker opponent (or be tromped by a much stronger one). We are challenged when we have a worthy opponent, one who brings out our best. Just think about how the level of play is elevated when evenly matched rivals with mutual respect compete against each other.

"Fierce and friendly" says it all. You try as hard as you can to win. If you knock down an opponent going for the ball, you grab the loose ball and try to score. But when the whistle blows, you help your opponent up. Sports gives us the chance to get to know people we compete with, even become friends with them, without ever letting up when the game is on.

Officials: Officials are integral as guides to fairness in the game. Honoring the Game means respecting officials even when they are wrong. There is never an excuse for treating officials with disrespect – no matter what.

Teammates: Never do anything, on or off the field, to embarrass your teammates. Honoring the Game involves behaving in a way that one's teammates, family, and community would be proud of.

Self: The foundation of Honoring the Game is respect for oneself. Individuals with self-respect would never dishonor the game because they have their own standards that they want to live up to – always.

I'm often asked if I expect people to Honor the Game when their opponents don't. *That's what having your own standards means.* Double-Goal Coaches and their athletes don't lower their standards because someone else does, even an opponent who gains an advantage. If you win by dishonoring the game, of what value is the victory?

Your Commitment to Honoring the Game

Coaches are positioned to have a dramatic and positive impact on their players, well beyond the playing field. If you make a commitment to teach and model Honoring the Game with your players, you can be part of the answer to our society's hungering need to elevate the way we treat each other. The next chapter contains practical tools you can use to do just that.

8

The Honoring the Game Toolkit

Many people talk a good game regarding sportsmanship, but the test is how one acts when it feels like something important is at stake. Behavior speaks louder than words. Harp at officials, and your players will also. Stay calm and focused, and they will emulate you. Thus your first task is to ensure you have the capacity to be an effective role model and teacher of Honoring the Game.

Prepare Yourself With a Self-Control Routine

You can't serve as a role model or effective teacher of Honoring the Game to your players if you have trouble controlling yourself when things go wrong. The calmest coach can be aggravated by a bad call or a player miscue at a crucial juncture of a game. Develop a self-control routine you can call on when provoked. To maintain or regain your composure, do one or more of the following:

- Take a deep breath or two.
- Turn away from the field to refocus.
- Count backwards from 100.
- Use self-talk. ("I need to be a role model for my players. I can rise above this.")

Prepare Your Players (and Their Parents) to "Keep a Cool Head"

Encourage your players and their parents to create their own self-control routine. Then in a game, when the temptation to lose one's temper increases, you can use a simple gesture to remind them to keep a cool head. You can use exactly the same speech to your players and their parents:

"When things start to get a little tense and I see any of you beginning to lose your cool, I'll just pat the top of my head a couple of times to remind you to keep a cool head. And you should give me or any members of our team the same signal if it looks like one of us is starting to lose it. We want to keep a cool head no matter what happens, so let's agree to remind each other when we are under pressure."

The remaining tools in this chapter can help you make Honoring the Game come alive for your players and for their parents.

Tools to Help Athletes Honor the Game

1 | Model and Teach Honoring the Game

Before your players can live up to the ROOTS of Honoring the Game, they will need to engage with the concept, again and again. One of the most important things you can do as a character-building coach is to introduce ROOTS early in the season and return to it throughout the season, ideally at least once every week.

Jot down some talking points to use with your players at an early practice and then return to them throughout the season. For example:

- I want us to Honor the Game so we can be proud of ourselves, win or lose.
- The acronym ROOTS will help us remember what we need to do.
- R – We obey the Rules even if we can get away with bending them, and even if our opponents don't.
- O – A worthy opponent helps us get better—we want to play fierce and friendly and never think of them as enemies.
- O – We respect officials even when bad calls go against us. I don't want you to confront officials during a game even if you are being treated unfairly.
- T – We don't do anything to embarrass our teammates, on or off the field.

- S for Self – Don't Honor the Game because I tell you to. Do it because you want to. We live up to our own standards even if our opponent doesn't.

Then periodically ask, "Who remembers what the R stands for? The O?" and so on.

2 | Seize Teachable Moments as They Arise

Use situations from your games or televised games as teachable moment conversation starters with players. If a high-profile coach or athlete has acted in a controversial way, ask your players if they think the behavior in question Honors the Game. Feel free to let them know what you think, but wait until they get their thoughts out. "I agree with Rashad. Taunting is not Honoring the Game nor is reacting violently when you are taunted. How can we make sure we don't respond if someone taunts us?"

Use positive examples as well. They aren't often highlighted in the media, but you will find many admirable actions by elite athletes you can use if you look for them.

3 | Make Your Point with Narrated Modeling

Just acting as a positive role model is not enough because people often misinterpret good behavior. Let's say the official has just made an obviously bad call. Because of your commitment to Honoring the Game, you remain silent. But your parents and players may think you don't know the rules or that you won't stick up for the team. So narrate what you are doing, both to your players and their parents so they won't miss the example you are setting for them.

"That was a bad call, but we Honor the Game on this team. And that means showing respect for officials even when they are wrong. So even though I was upset by the call, I waited until a time-out, and then I respectfully asked about it."

4 | Drill Honoring the Game in Practice

As coaches, we would never expect players to implement a new defense in a game without lots of practice. We practice it over and over until they get it. Do the same with Honoring the Game. Have them practice reacting the right way to tough situations before they confront them in a game. Here are some ways to do that:

- Officiate a scrimmage or competition in practice and make a flagrantly bad call. When the aggrieved player reacts in anger, use it as a teachable moment. "Is an official ever going to make a bad call in a game? (Yes.) Are you going to lose control in a game the way you did just now? (No.) Good!"

- Have players try to make a play or a shot while a teammate is distracting them verbally. (Make sure they understand not to talk trash or say anything mean-spirited.) This will increase their concentration, and you can use it to explain that you want them to keep their focus even if an opponent taunts them.

- Have players officiate a practice scrimmage. They will be amazed how difficult it is to get every call right, which will help them empathize with the officials.

- Invite officials to come to your practice and talk about how they do their job.

Tools to Help Parents to Honor the Game

Prevention is the best cure. Coaches who create a team culture based on Honoring the Game will have fewer sidelines problems among parents. Here's how to do that.

1 | Set expectations with a parent meeting.

Set the tone for the behavior you expect at a meeting with parents before competitions start. Distribute a letter explaining PCA principles (ELM Tree of Mastery, Filling the Emotional Tank, Honoring the Game). Review these principles with parents, and specifically ask them for their support to teach and model them to the players. Ask them to sign the PCA Parent Pledge, which along with a sample Parent/Guardian Letter and a Parent/Guardian Meeting Agenda, are available on PCA's website (see page 70).

2 | Appoint a "Culture Keeper."

Appoint a parent as your team's Culture Keeper to help with sideline management. The ideal Culture Keeper is outgoing and able to remind parents to Honor the Game without further riling them. Or, rotate the job so that, over time, every parent has experience being a Culture Keeper. Check in with your Culture Keeper before each game to make sure they say hello to each parent and remind them to set a positive example by Honoring the Game. A Culture Keeper handout with detailed information on this role is available on PCA's website (see page 70).

3 | Cue parents before high-stakes games.

A playoff game is more likely to prompt bad behavior than an early-season game. Cue parents before high-stakes games, including reminding them of the signal for "Keeping a Cool Head" introduced earlier in this chapter. "Today's game is important, and we want to play our best. I want to remind you to Honor the Game today. If there is a bad call by the official, I want you to be silent – it's my job to address it. Your job is to fill players' E-Tanks and be role models who Honor the Game."

4 | Routinely introduce officials to your parents.

When you can, introduce officials to your parents. "This is Hector Garcia and Heather Stanley. They'll be calling the game today, and I know we all want to show them the respect they deserve. Let's thank them for being willing to do a tough job."

5 | Nip problems in the bud.

Sometimes the best prevention fails and you need to intervene. The earlier you respond to bad sideline behavior, the less likely it will get out of control. Like a match dropping in a forest, it's relatively easy to put out a fire at first, but it gets much harder once the blaze is going. Respond at the first sign of misbehavior. "Okay, cool it. I need you to Honor the Game and not distract or embarrass our players." Sometimes just a look and "Keep-a-Cool-Head" gesture will do the job. Some guidelines for intervening:

- **Stay calm:** To paraphrase Rudyard Kipling: If you can keep your head while all around you others are losing theirs…you'll get better results. Getting upset at parents who are already upset can add fuel to the fire. Be firm but calm. And if you can't be totally calm, be as calm as you can be.

- **Respect personal space:** When a person's zone of personal space is entered without permission, it activates self-protection instincts and can easily lead to escalation. Avoid getting in someone's face when prompting him to behave. Stay at least arm's length away, and avoid any threatening manner.

- **Empathize:** Sometimes it helps to recognize the difficulty of what you are asking. "It's not easy to remain silent when the official makes a call that you don't like, but it's important that we're good role models."

- **Invoke a higher standard:** People tend to respond to a higher standard. Remind them of your team's commitment to Honor the Game. Reference the Parent Pledge (mentioned on page 49). "Remember the pledge you signed? You agreed to Honor the Game even when there is a bad call. That's what I need you to do right now."

- **Perfection not required:** You can stammer; the words can come out wrong; you can be abrupt. That's okay. You don't have to intervene perfectly. But you do need to intervene. Coaches have a responsibility to defend the positive sports culture we want for our children. You are the leader of the team, so let parents and fans know what is acceptable and what is not.

- **When all else fails:** Sometimes no matter how well you handle a situation, it still gets out of control. If you feel you have done all you can to get parents to behave without success, ask leaders of your organization to help resolve the situation.

CHAPTER NINE

Case Studies for Double-Goal Coaches

PCA is an organization of coaches and athletes who collectively have experienced almost every kind of situation one can imagine on the playing field. The cases in this chapter address frequent situations in which coaches find themselves. They give you the chance to "practice" how as a Double-Goal you might respond to these situations before you encounter them for real in the heat of the moment.

You'll get the most from these case studies if you decide on your response before you read my suggestions. Jotting your thoughts down first is even better. Keep in mind that while my thoughts on the case studies are informed by some of the best coaching minds, all athletes and teams are different, so no one size fits all.

1 | Sideline Confrontation

In a crucial situation near the end of a tight game against a strong opponent, the official makes a call against your team that appears wrong. Two parents of your players, outraged by the call, begin to yell at the officials. Your team loses narrowly. The parents continue to scream at the official while your players look to you expectantly. As a Double-Goal Coach, what should you do?

As bad as things are, they can get much worse. Your first priority is reining in your outraged parents. And I do mean "your" parents. Parents come with players, and it is your responsibility to shape their behavior as well as that of your players. Here's how:

- If you have an assistant coach, have him take players to a meeting place away from the field. If you are the only coach present, ask your captains to gather the team at a meeting place and wait for you there.

- Approach the yelling parents to quiet them down. Be firm without causing any further escalation. "I need you to leave the officials alone right now!"

- Empathize with the parents while reminding them that they are violating your team culture of Honoring the Game. "I know that was a tough call to take, but I need you to stop and set an example for our team." If Honoring the Game is part of your team culture, remind them now. "Remember, we're a team that Honors the Game. We've got to live up to that now."

- Thank the officials. If you agree that the bad call may have cost your team the game, this may be hard, but it would be a big Honoring-the-Game statement. "Thank you for officiating today. I know this is often a thankless job. I want you to know I will speak to my parents to make sure they don't act this way in the future."

- Address your team, ideally within earshot of the parents so you can talk to them through your remarks to the players. This is a great time to remind your players that they played a good game. Don't let the controversial call overshadow their great effort. "We had a tough call at the end of the game, but I was proud of the way you kept compet- ing. In life we don't always get the right calls, but competitors don't whine about it – they refocus on the next play. And that's what you did today."

- End by recommitting to Honoring the Game. "We're a team that shows respect for officials even when they mess up. Thank you for not harping on them today."

- Before the next game, talk to the parents in question to ensure they are prepared to behave themselves in the future. Wait for the emotion to dissipate, but do talk with them so they know you expect them to Honor the Game in the future.

2 | Nerves and the Big Game

All week long you've had trouble getting your athletes to focus. You think they are nervous about their upcoming competition against a powerful, undefeated team. You have a few minutes with your athletes before the competition starts to get them ready to compete. As a Double-Goal Coach, what can you say?

Your goal is to prepare them to compete at their best. If the other team has more talent, victory on the scoreboard may not be realistic. On the other hand, a team playing to its fullest potential can often surprise.

At times like these, when the stakes seem high, the most committed Double-Goal Coach may be tempted to focus on a scoreboard win. *Resist that temptation.* You'll get better scoreboard results if you re-emphasize the ELM Tree with your players before a big game. "I know you'd like to win today. So would I, but let's keep our focus on the ELM Tree, which gives us the best chance to win. Leave everything you have out on the field. Keep learning things that will make us better. Flush your mistakes, and focus on the next play. If we do, we'll be winners no matter what the score is at the end." Here are other thoughts:

- Encourage them to have fun. "The pressure is on them. Everyone expects them to win. We've nothing to lose. So let's have fun going all out!"

- Remind them of their preparation. "You've worked hard all week. We have a plan, so let's focus on doing what we know how to do."

- Nervous is normal (and good!). "How many of you are nervous today? Good! If you weren't, I'd be worried that you didn't care about today's game. I'm glad you're nervous. Now let's use that energy to play our game today."

- Pressure is a privilege. "We're lucky we get to play in a big game! Many people go through their entire life without experiencing what we'll experience today. So let's give it our best effort and have fun while we're at it!"

3 | Time Crunch with Practice Coming

Coaching is taking more time than you thought, especially planning practices. You worry about doing justice to both your job and your coaching. As a Double-Goal Coach, how can you get more efficient at practice planning?

Designing dynamic practices is an art many experienced coaches haven't mastered. Effective practices are a huge motivational boost to players and contribute to building a successful team. Here are ways to make the most of practices.

- Use a transition ritual to get into a proper coaching attitude. I often left work thinking about tasks I hadn't finished, and not in a frame of mind to give my players the positive energy they deserved. In the parking lot I would say to myself, "I get to coach basketball today!" When I was able to say this with enthusiasm and mean it, I entered the gym excited to be with my players.

- Build practices around core activities to keep from having to create a unique plan for each practice. This keeps the focus on fundamentals throughout the season, reduces wasted energy as players learn a routine which requires less explanation, and focuses players' energy on learning new things while routine things get done efficiently as part of the core. Some core activities to make part of every practice.

✓ Objectives and Priorities	✓ Scrimmaging
✓ Opening Ritual	✓ Fun Activities
✓ Instruction	✓ Team Conversations
✓ Skill Drills	✓ Closing Ritual
✓ Conditioning	✓ Assessment

- Write your plan. In a crunch a bad written plan is better than the best unwritten plan. It doesn't have to be elaborate. Even five minutes to jot down bullet points with estimated times for each activity you want to do will help.

- Make safety a priority. Check out the field to ensure safe conditions. Have a first-aid kit, cell phone, and parent contact information available in case of emergency. Learn about hydration needs and ensure adequate hydration, especially in hot weather. If yours is a contact sport, learn about concussions and how to deal with players who may have experienced one.

- Use an opening ritual to start each practice the same way to help players get ready to focus and work hard. I like to use an activity that gets them moving and working together rather than forcing them to be stationary and listen to me right off the bat. If you can find a way to make this opening ritual something the players love doing, then they are even more motivated to get to practice on time (or early)! One high school soccer coach started each practice with juggling (for team and personal records), and he usually had all of his players there with their equipment on five minutes before the official start time of practice.

- Share your top priorities for each practice with players in a quick team conversation and/or by e-mailing them or posting them on a team website for your players to see. Think about what your players need to be successful in upcoming games and spend time on that – with instruction, drills, and scrimmaging.

- Mix up practice activities for a change of pace. Use a pattern of teach-drill-scrimmage so players don't have to sit still listening for a long time before they get to try a skill and use it in a game-like situation.

- Make adjustments. If you planned 10 minutes for a drill but more work is needed on it, you can extend the drill, recognizing that something else will have to give. A written plan makes this easier to do.

- Hold short, frequent team conversations. Multiple conversations of two minutes or less throughout a practice are superior to a long team meeting of 10 minutes or more. As coaches, we often fall into the trap of talking for long periods of time, when, in fact, what our athletes need most is time playing. Make the short conversations two-way. Ask questions to get players talking, thinking, and learning. The ideal time for a team conversation is after a conditioning drill. Tired players appreciate a coach's message while they catch their breath.

- Use a closing ritual to help players reenter their daily lives. It might be a quick conversation about how practice went or one thing they can take from it to their schoolwork, their families, and such. End a practice on a high note so they are excited about the upcoming game or the next practice. I often ended practice doing short visualization exercises that my players loved. Some teams use a high-energy cheer.

- On the way home, review what happened and formulate your priorities for the next practice while this one is fresh in your mind.

4 | Disruptive Kids

Some of your players have short attention spans and frequently disrupt team conversations and drills. Most players pay attention and do what you ask but seem as frustrated as you. As a Double-Goal Coach, what can you do?

Every coach at every level has players who misbehave, goof off, or lack focus during practice. Here are three basic principles for shaping the behavior of your players.

1. **Reinforce desired behavior.** Attention, good or bad, can reinforce behavior you *don't* want. As strange as it may seem, yelling at a kid can reinforce inappropriate behavior. Give attention to kids when they do what you want. Thank those who respond right away: "Artemio, Jalmer, Nico, thanks for hustling in!" Tie their cooperation to the team's success. "With limited practice time, it really helps when you come right away!"

2. **Ignore undesired behavior.** Vic *didn't* come when you called, so ignore him. Until he does what you want, Vic doesn't exist (actually you keep an eye on him so he doesn't get hurt). When Vic realizes he can't get your attention by misbehaving, he'll likely try to get it by complying. When he does, reward him: "Vic, thanks for doing what I asked!" This tends to work like magic, but not always, so read on.

3. **When you can't ignore, intervene in a least-attention manner.** Sometimes you can't ignore behavior – a player may put herself in danger or disrupt your practice – so intervene in a "least-attention manner." "Tina, I need you to sit here until you can follow my

directions. When you're ready to do what I ask, you can rejoin the team." If this doesn't work, add a check-in. "Tina, sit here. I'll be back shortly to see if you are ready to rejoin the team." This is a great time for a fun activity that Tina will miss. Before she can rejoin the team, have her acknowledge what she needs to do. "Tina, can you follow my direction now?" She has to agree before you let her rejoin the team, even if it's just a head nod.

As a basketball coach, I made sure every player had his own ball. When I wanted their attention, I said, "Hold the balls." If a player didn't, I calmly took it. If he got upset, I said, "When you learn to hold your ball when I'm talking, you can keep it." This worked like a charm.

These principles are simple but not easy. It's all too easy to get angry at misbehavior and ignoring misbehavior can feel unnatural. But if followed, these three principles will help you regain control of your team. Here are some other thoughts:

- Get to know your players as individuals. Learn their names and interests and make a connection as quickly as you can. Smile and greet each player by name at the start and end of every practice.

- Keep the three C's in mind: Calmness, Consequences, and Consistency. You'll get much farther with Calmness than anger. A calm correction connected to a Consequence works far better than a shout. And Consistency in applying consequences helps players come to understand what is expected of them.

- The best defense is a good offense. Kids engaged in purposeful and fun activities are far less likely to misbehave.

- Keep rules simple, especially with younger kids. For them, these three rules can cover almost anything: 1) Give your best effort, 2) Support your teammates, and 3) Listen when coaches talk.

- Involve older players in developing team rules at the beginning of the season. Get their agreement, including the consequences for violating them. Then when there is a violation, you can remind them of their commitment to obey the rules and the consequences that you established together.

- Get your assistants on the same page. Your effectiveness at managing player behavior is undercut if they give attention to undesirable behavior.

- Consider making an especially difficult child Player of the Day (see page 37).

5 | Wildly Varying Abilities

You have a wide range of ability on your team. A couple of players are stars and could compete well in a higher age group. Many players are average and a few are very raw. You've noticed the better players criticizing weaker ones. How do you forge these players of wildly varying abilities into a real team?

Much of American youth sports seems determined to emulate the old East German system and channel players by ability as early as possible. Nonetheless, almost every team at every level has players of differing abilities, and the best coaches get good production from their "role players." Here are some ideas for building this group into a real team.

- Set team goals. The best team-builder is a goal that excites every member of the team. Think about a goal (like winning a league title or being the hardest-working team in the league) that is a just-right challenge for the team. When superstars see that every team member is required to achieve the goal, they'll be more likely to support the other players.

- Preach the message of the Home Team Advantage. Emphasize the importance of filling E-Tanks to get teammates to perform their best.

- Get your top players to lead. Stanford women's basketball coach Tara VanDerveer once told me the key to a hard-working team: "The best players have to be the hardest workers." Convince your best players of this, and they will set a standard for the entire team.

- Enlist your best players as teachers. Tell them if they learn something well enough to teach it, it will help them when they get to the next level. Work with them before or after practice on how to teach a skill while emphasizing their need to fill the E-Tanks of the players they are teaching. Then have them help other players learn it. You can also get all your players teaching each other with the following procedure.

  1) Explain and demonstrate a skill to the entire group.

  2) Pair players up to demonstrate the skill to each other. Encourage them to fill each others' E-Tanks as they work together.

  3) Intervene with those pairs who need more instruction. Give feedback out of ear-shot of others; the pair will be more open to it than if given in front of everyone.

  4) Ask for volunteers to demonstrate the skill in front of everyone.

- Help every player set effort goals that are "Just-Right Challenges" (see page 27). If the better players are challenged, they will use their energy to try to meet the challenge rather than putting down teammates.

- Intentionally raise the profile of "role" players. Make a point of calling out their contributions, especially their effort, in team conversation. Structure team conversations so you hear from everyone, not just the stars or the most vocal players.

6 | Coaching Your Own Child

You have the chance to coach your own child. As a Double-Goal Coach, how can you make it a great experience for everyone involved with the team?

Historically, young people have apprenticed with their parents' business. My father talked with great joy about going to work in the fields of the family farm with my grandfather at the age of 12. Today there is little opportunity for this, but coaching your own child can be a wonderful experience in working together. Many parents and children look back on their times together on a sports team as some of the best moments of their lives. Here are some tips for making that shared experience a positive one.

- Ask your child. "How would you feel about me coaching your team this season?" If he has reservations, it's good to know that up front. If they are strong ones, you may want to choose to be a supportive sports parent, not "coach," this season.

- Recognize that you wear two hats. Tell your child you need to treat her like everyone else on the team when you wear your coach's hat. It helps when your child calls you "coach" during practices and games, not mom or dad. But when you put your parent hat on, she is the most important person in your life (along with other family members). Some parent-coaches even wear a special coaching cap. After a game or practice, they make a point of changing hats: "I'm taking my coach hat off and putting my dad hat on."

- Be sensitive to favoring or penalizing your child. Many coaches give their child advantages (like starting games or playing favored positions) the child hasn't "earned" by effort or talent. Few things poison the well with other parents and players like a coach unfairly favoring his own child. However, many coaches are *harder* on their own child. It's difficult to be objective about our own child, so you may find it useful to ask another person (perhaps an assistant coach) to let you know if you are treating your own child fairly compared to other players on your team.

- If you have an assistant coach, you might find it useful to regularly have him or her give instruction and feedback to your child while you return the favor.

- Don't talk about other players on the team with your child. This places him in a complicated situation and may color his relationships with other players. He is a member of the team, not your co-coach.

- Avoid sports overload with your child by doing non-sport family activities during the season. If doing sports at home, focus on having fun rather than on drills designed to make your child better. This way she will be fresh for practice rather than feeling she gets no respite from sports.

- Use PCA tools like Kid-Friendly Criticism, Asking Permission, and If-Then Statements, (see page 40) that are especially helpful to parent-coaches because they enable athletes to hear and embrace criticism rather than become defensive.

Your time coaching your child will pass by very quickly. Whatever happens, I encourage you to stay in the moment and enjoy this special time.

7 | Making Parents an Asset

The last time you coached, parents were a negative influence that kept your team from achieving its potential. It's a new season with new players and parents. As a Double-Goal Coach, what can you do to avoid a repeat of last season?

Some coaches only want to coach kids, not deal with unruly or unreasonable parents. But kids bring parents with them. Here's how to make parents an asset to your team. (Note: The Appendix has a list of related resources.)

- When your team has been formed, call players to tell them you are excited they are on your team. Then ask to speak to their mom or dad. Tell the parent that you look forward to working with them to help their child have a terrific experience this season, and that you will soon send a letter or e-mail explaining your Double-Goal coaching philosophy.

- Use a parent meeting to review the principles of Double-Goal Coaching (ELM Tree of Mastery, Filling Emotional Tanks, and Honoring the Game). Ask them to promote these ideas with the team. Tell them you know your team will get bad calls, but ask them to commit to Honoring the Game no matter what.

- Explain that the Emotional Tank and the ELM Tree of Mastery are research-based concepts that are keys to their child's performance. Ask them to fill E-Tanks and reinforce the ELM Tree with their child throughout the season.

- Hand out the PCA Parent Pledge available on the PCA website (see page 70). After you have reviewed the document, ask them if they have any questions. Then ask them to sign it.

- Recruit "Culture Keepers" (see page 50) for the team who will work to keep other parents positive on the sidelines during games.

- When in doubt, communicate. Coaches run into problems when they assume parents understand why they coach the way they do. Don't assume. If you have rules about playing time or missing practice, for example, tell them. Ask them to contact you with concerns rather than share them with their child. Give them your contact information and let them know when to talk with you (e.g., not right before practice). Over-communicating will save you time over the course of the season, and it will enhance your players' experience.

- Fill parents' E-Tanks with truthful and specific praise when they do something positive. Thank them for helping you build a positive team culture. Try to tell them something positive about their child every time you see them (again being truthful and specific). If you do, they will think you are a genius as a coach!

8 | Playing Time Blues

You coach a competitive team in which playing time is not guaranteed but earned. You have players (and parents) who grumble about not getting to play as much as they'd like. As a Double-Goal Coach, what can you do?

Let me say right off that good coaches get players into games. They may be creative about how to do it in high-stakes situations, but good coaches – Double-Goal Coaches – get kids into games.

Lack of playing time for their kids is probably the biggest source of frustration and anger among sports parents, so this is worth your attention as it can eat away at team solidarity. Save yourself a lot of grief by making your playing time policy clear before athletes join your team. Parents and players may still be unhappy about playing time decisions, but at least they will have been forewarned.

But having done that doesn't get you off the hook for getting all your players into games. Kids love to play. They don't like to sit on the bench.

Most of the benefits of sports are tied to competing in games. Kids who sit benefit less from sports than kids who play. And lack of playing time is a big reason kids drop out of sports, which, to a Double-Goal Coach, is a tragedy.

Here are some strategies for getting more kids into games.

- If coaching elementary-aged kids in a recreation league, give all kids equal playing time even if the league doesn't mandate it. The primary goal coaching young athletes should be to have fun and help them develop a love of the game. This comes from playing, not watching.

- With middle and high school kids, tell players you reward effort and then do it. Reward high-effort players with playing time, independent of ability. Players will realize that they don't have to be as talented as the best players to get into games, they just have to outwork them! This is incredibly motivating to your weaker players. And it is a wake-up call for stronger players who will up their effort level to stay in games longer.

- Use blowout games to get kids into games *before* the game becomes a blowout. Look for mismatches coming up and start kids who normally don't start. If that puts your team behind, the starters coming into the game will have to work harder to catch up, which is good for them. If the subs outscore the opponent, they will have the satisfaction of doing it when the game was still up for grabs.

- In high-stakes games with older players where you know some players are unlikely to play much, prepare them. "We're playing a tough team this week, so you may not get in much, but you'll play more next week. Keep working hard in practice so you're ready when we need you."

- Coach all players including those on the bench. Talk about what's going on in the game. Have them watch for things that can help the team. Have them do Positive Charting (see page 39). Involve all your players, and you'll have a more cohesive team and players will work harder because they feel a stake in the team.

- Get creative like this high school basketball coach did. On a 12-person team, he called his bottom five players the "Mad Dogs." The Mad Dogs knew they would play the last minute of the first quarter and the first minute of the second quarter in every game, whether pre-season or the state title game.

Unlike typical bench players, the Mad Dogs worked extremely hard in practice because they wanted to be ready for their moment. This pushed the starters to play harder in practice. They played all out during their two minutes. They were all over the court and were highly aggressive. Over time, they became a competitive advantage, with the team being in a better competitive position after the Mad Dogs came out.

The Mad Dogs developed increased self-confidence and a sense of possibility for themselves that helped some of them become starters. And when an individual latches onto a sense of possibility, watch out! Getting every player into every game helped this entire team perform better. So getting players into games is not just for their individual benefit. It ups the effort level – and ultimately the success – of your entire team.

9 | Losing Badly (and Well)

Your team is consistently overmatched in games. You've lost your first few games convincingly, and you fear you might be looking at a no-win season. You get embarrassed and frustrated during games. As a Double-Goal Coach, how do you motivate players to maintain effort and improve in the face of a string of blowout losses?

It's not easy to keep our composure in the public fishbowl of one-sided losses. But it is worth remembering that it is often when things go wrong that Double-Goal Coaches can have the most impact.

Here are some strategies for dealing with this challenge:

• Prepare yourself. Tell yourself you are going to be upbeat throughout the game no matter what. Visualize yourself encouraging players when they do something right. Stay positive in your verbal comments to fill their Emotional Tanks, which are going to drain as they get behind. Make this about giving your players what they need to keep playing hard rather than about how embarrassed you are by the scoreboard.

- Establish your game face and keep it on throughout the game. Your game face (which includes your posture) should be of a coach who is proud of his players and continues to coach and teach throughout the game. Emulate the great coaches who outwardly react the same to a touchdown by their team as to an interception by the other team.

- Remember that a mastery approach works in blowouts as well as tight games. Remind players constantly of the ELM Tree. Reinforce those who try hard against more talented players. Focus on the improvement individuals and the team are making.

- Use Effort Goals to give your players something within their reach to shoot for. See page 25 for how one coach "moved the goal posts" to keep his players motivated throughout a no-win season.

- Break each game into bite-size chunks of time.
    - ✓ "Let's see if we can tie or win this inning!"
    - ✓ "Let's give it everything we've got for the last three minutes of the half."

If you do, you may be pleasantly surprised by the end of the season. I once got my baseball team to adopt an inning-by-inning focus after we fell behind 6-0 in the first inning of a playoff game. We tied a couple of innings and even won one although we lost the game badly. We won our way through the loser's bracket to come within one game of playing that same team again for the championship, losing to a talented team in extra innings.

- Endorse yourself after a loss for being a Double-Goal Coach who helps players learn to persevere in the face of adversity. That is a lot more important (and harder) than coaching a team that wins easily and often.

10 | Using Assistant Coaches Effectively

At first you were glad to have a couple of parents help you coach this season. But now they seem more trouble than they are worth. You're not really sure how to use them to help the team get better. As a

Double-Goal Coach, how can you integrate assistants so they add value to your players and team?

Our society's mythology glorifies the individual leader, but great organizations are usually led by leadership teams. Sports teams are no different. Forge your assistant coaches into a cohesive leadership team, and you will accomplish much more. And you will address a huge problem with youth sports practices – too many kids standing around.

The tradeoff is control versus reach. If you do all the coaching, you can do it to your standards. However, integrating assistants into your leadership team will extend your impact on your players. But that requires delegating, something many coaches either aren't willing or don't know how to do. Here are some thoughts about how to do this well:

- Familiarize assistants with your Double-Goal coaching philosophy by using the Double-Goal Coach Job Description (see page 70). Get their commitment to help build the team culture you want before empowering them.

- Assign them to fill E-Tanks of all players in early practices and ask them to share what they did. Make overlooked players the focus of the next practice. Make your assistants tank fillers, and it will have a huge impact on your team.

- Here are three ways to delegate to assistant coaches:

    1. **See and Do:** Assistant watches you teach a skill and replicates it with another group of players.

    2. **Plan and Preview:** Assistant plans to teach a specific skill at an upcoming practice and previews it with you before trying it out on the players.

    3. **Do and Report:** Assistant teaches a skill to part of the team and reports how well it went.

- Involve assistants in practice planning and carve out active roles for them in games.

Create a strong leadership team and you also prepare your assistants as Double-Goal Coaches who will go on to positively impact many youth as head coaches in the future.

10

Your Legacy as a Coach Revisited

Much of what we do in life doesn't seem to leave much of a trail. We can work hard for a long time without much visible impact.

But coaching is a place where we can see our impact.

And if we are Double-Goal Coaches, we see it both in how our athletes compete and how they turn out as adults. If during their time with you, your players learn to embrace the ELM Tree of Mastery, fill Emotional Tanks of those around them, and Honor the Game, they will be successful in their career, family life, and the larger community. They will be contributing citizens of which you, and our country, can be proud.

Someone told me years ago that there is little in life as satisfying as being part of someone else's success. Coaches are ideally positioned to be part of their players' success, perhaps more so than any other adult other than parents.

This book and Positive Coaching Alliance are intended to support you to be the kind of coach who makes a lifetime of difference.

But I want to challenge you to go beyond your individual influence as a coach to have an even bigger impact on our nation's youth. By joining the PCA Movement, you become part of a virtual team that is committed to transforming youth sports so sports can transform youth.

And because sports has so much symbolic importance in this society, if we transform youth sports, we will transform the entire society. That's how important PCA's mission is.

Here are a few ways you can help extend the PCA Movement.

- Continue learning to become the very best Double-Goal Coach you can be. PCA has multiple live and on-line workshops and books that go beyond the material in this book.

- Sign up for the *PCA Connector,* our weekly electronic newsletter with tips and other useful information.

- Become a Positive Coaching Alliance member.

- Tell others about PCA. If you have friends and relatives involved with youth sports, perhaps in other parts of the country (or world), refer them to PCA's web site.

- Encourage your schools and youth sports organizations to partner with PCA.

Information on all of the above is available at www.positivecoach.org, by calling (toll-free) 866-725-0024, by e-mail at pca@positivecoach.org, or by mail at Positive Coaching Alliance, 1001 N. Rengstorff Avenue, Mountain View, CA 94043.

John W. Gardner, once said, "Meaning is not something you stumble across, like the answer to a riddle or the prize in a treasure hunt. Meaning is something you build into your life."

Being a Double-Goal Coach in the lives of youth athletes is a sure-fire way of building meaning into your life. It will enrich their lives and yours. That is my wish for you and all the athletes you coach.

Appendix

Here are some of the many resources and tools available at www.positivecoach.org.

- **Parent-Guardian Meeting Agenda:** Hold a parent meeting before the season starts to explain your Double-Goal Coaching principles.

- **Parent-Guardian Letter:** Use this to introduce Double-Goal Coaching to parents at a meeting, or send it via e-mail or home with players after the first practice.

- **Parent Pledge:** Review this pledge with parents and have them sign it to reinforce the messages you want to send your players.

- **Culture Keeper Job Description:** Use this to recruit one or more parents as Culture Keepers on the sidelines during games to help parents support the team culture you want to create.

- **Double-Goal Coach Job Description:** Share this with assistant coaches to get them on the same page as you.

- **Positive Charting:** This powerful tool includes directions and a form to reinforce the positive things you see your athletes doing.

- **Positive Coaching Scripts and Talking Points:** Use Scripts to introduce Double-Goal Coaching principles to your players. Use Talking Points to reinforce the ELM Tree, Emotional Tank, and Honoring the Game throughout the season.

- **Online Workshops:** The PCA web site offers interactive online workshops for coaches, parents, and athletes featuring video of PCA National Advisory Board members (Phil Jackson, Doc Rivers, Carol Dweck, and others).

Workshop Evaluation | Coaching for Winning and Life Lessons

Date: _____

Presenter: _____

Your Organization: _____

Gender: ☐ Male   ☐ Female   Your Age: _____

Ethnicity: ☐ White   ☐ African-American

☐ Latino   ☐ Asian-American   ☐ Other

Years coaching experience:_____   Are you a parent? ☐ Yes ☐ No

Sports you coach:_____

Age group you coach: _____

To help us do a better job, we need your feedback. Thank you very much!
Please circle your response indicating your selection.

		POOR	AVERAGE		EXCELLENT	
1.	Overall workshop	1	2	3	4	5
2.	Presenter's effectiveness	1	2	3	4	5
3.	Content of the workshop	1	2	3	4	5
4.	Length of the workshop ☐ Too Short ☐ Just Right ☐ Too Long					

		NOT AT ALL			VERY WELL	
5.	Did your presenter clearly explain PCA's three key principles and the corresponding coaching tools for each?	1	2	3	4	5
6.	Did your presenter keep you engaged during the workshop?	1	2	3	4	5
7.	I would recommend this workshop to other coaches	1	2	3	4	5

		DISAGREE			AGREE	
8.	I intend to use workshop material this year	1	2	3	4	5

9. The best part of this workshop was: _____

_____

10. A way to improve this workshop is: _____

_____

Become a PCA Member Today!

For as little as $25 per year, you can help PCA make a difference in the lives of hundreds of thousands of athletes every year!

As a member, you will be invited to hear podcasts and webinar discussions featuring top athletes and coaches like Summer Sanders, Doc Rivers, and Steve Young. You'll also get a Triple-Impact Competitor Bag Tag to give to a student-athlete!

Yes, I want to make a difference in youth sports by donating:

☐ $25

☐ Other Amount

Your Name _____

Street Address _____

City, State, Zip _____

Phone_____

Email _____

☐ Please make my gift anonymous

☐ I/We work for a matching gift company

To sign up online, visit **http://donate.positivecoach.org/Membership**

Or mail this form to:

Positive Coaching Alliance
Attn: Membership
1001 N. Rengstorff Ave., Suite 100
Mountain View, CA 94043